ENDANGERED
ANIMALS OF THE
ISLANDS

Barbara J. Behm
Jean-Christophe Balouet

For a free color catalog describing Gareth Stevens' list
of high-quality books, call 1-800-542-2595 (USA) or
1-800-461-9120 (Canada). Gareth Stevens' Fax: (414) 225-0377.

The editor would like to extend special thanks to Jan W. Rafert, Curator of Primates
and Small Mammals, Milwaukee County Zoo, Milwaukee, Wisconsin, for his kind
and professional help with the information in this book.

Library of Congress Cataloging-in-Publication Data

Behm, Barbara, 1952-
    Endangered animals of the islands/by Barbara J. Behm and Jean-Christophe Balouet.
       p. cm. -- (In peril)
    "Adapted from Ces espèces qui disparaissent . . . with original text by Jean-Christophe
Balouet"--T.p. verso.
    Includes bibliographical references (p. 30) and index.
    ISBN 0-8368-1078-3
    1. Endangered species--Juvenile literature.   2. Island fauna--Juvenile literature.   [1.
Endangered species.]   I. Balouet, Jean-Christophe.   Ces espèces qui disparaissent.   II.
Title.   III. Series: Behm, Barbara, 1952- In peril.
    QL83.B445   1994
    591.52'9'09142--dc20   94-11676

This edition first published in 1994 by
Gareth Stevens Publishing
1555 North RiverCenter Drive, Suite 201
Milwaukee, Wisconsin 53212, USA

This edition © 1994 by Gareth Stevens, Inc. Adapted from *Ces Espèces qui Disparaissent,*
© 1990 by Editions Ouest-France, with original text by Jean-Christophe Balouet. This
edition published by arrangement with David Bateman, Ltd. Additional end matter
© 1994 by Gareth Stevens, Inc.

Picture Credits
André Aaron (with the courtesy of the Mammals and Birds Laboratory of the National
Museum of Natural History of Paris): pp. 7, 13 (lower), 17, 18, 24 (upper), 25; Roger Bour:
p. 22; Jean-Pierre Djivanides: p. 5; Jacana: Cover, pp. 6, 19, 20, 26, 27, 28; National
Library: pp. 8, 11, 14, 21, 24 (lower); Central Library Museum, National Museum of Natural
History of Paris: pp. 9, 23; Photo Researchers: p. 10; Douglas Pratt: pp. 13 (upper), 15, 16;
Pritchard: p. 12

Series logo artwork: Tom Redman

Series editor: Patricia Lantier-Sampon
Series designer: Karen Knutson
Research assistants: Diane Laska, Derek Smith
Translated from the French by: Anne-Marie Jardon-Sampont
Map art: Donna Genzmer Schenström, University of Wisconsin-Milwaukee Cartographic
    Services Laboratory

Printed in the United States of America

 2 3 4 5 6 7 8 9 99 98 97 96 95

At this time, Gareth Stevens, Inc., does not use 100 percent recycled paper, although the
paper used in our books does contain about 30 percent recycled fiber. This decision was
made after a careful study of current recycling procedures revealed their dubious
environmental benefits. We will continue to explore recycling options.

INTRODUCTION

For millions of years, during the course of evolution, hundreds of plant and animal species have appeared on Earth, multiplied, and then, for a variety of reasons, vanished. We all know of animals today — such as the elephant and the rhinoceros, the mountain gorilla and the orangutan — that face extinction because of irresponsible human activity or changes in environmental conditions. Amazingly, hundreds of species of insects and plants become extinct before we can even classify them. Fortunately, in modern times, we are beginning to understand that all living things are connected. When we destroy a plant species, we may be depriving the world of an amazing cure for human diseases. And we know that if we destroy the forest, the desert creeps forward and the climate changes, wild animals die off because they cannot survive the harsh conditions, and humans, too, face starvation and death. Let us remember that every creature and plant is part of a web of life, each perfect, each contributing to the whole. It is up to each of us to end the destruction of our natural world before it becomes too late. Future generations will find it hard to forgive us if we fail to act. No matter what our age or where we live, it is time for every one of us to get involved.

Dr. Jane Goodall, Ethologist

CONTENTS

Words that appear in the glossary are printed in **boldface** type the first time they occur in the text.

ISLANDS

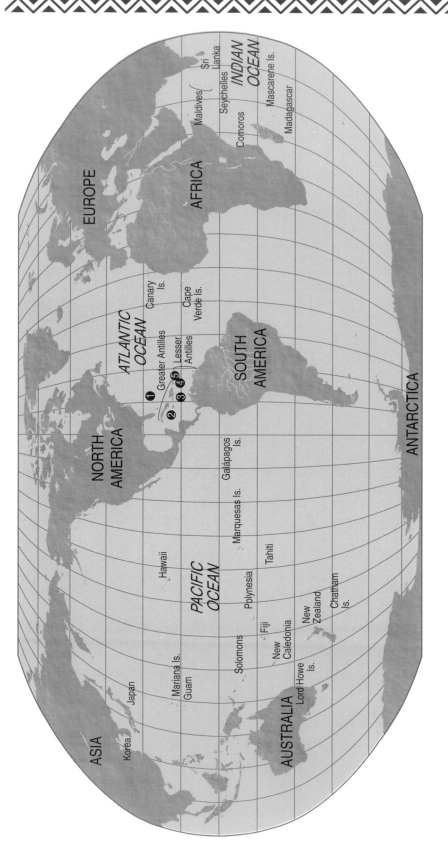

The map shows the following labeled locations:

- ASIA
- Korea
- Japan
- EUROPE
- NORTH AMERICA
- Mariana Is.
- Guam
- Hawaii
- Solomons
- Fiji
- New Caledonia
- PACIFIC OCEAN
- Polynesia
- Marquesas Is.
- Tahiti
- New Zealand
- Chatham Is.
- Lord Howe Is.
- AUSTRALIA
- Galápagos Is.
- Canary Is.
- ATLANTIC OCEAN
- Greater Antilles
- Lesser Antilles
- Cape Verde Is.
- SOUTH AMERICA
- AFRICA
- Maldives
- Sri Lanka
- Seychelles
- Comoros
- INDIAN OCEAN
- Mascarene Is.
- Madagascar
- ANTARCTICA

▲ For various reasons, many species of plant and animal life on Earth are in great peril of disappearing forever. Unfortunately, this danger is not limited to any one place; it has become a global problem. From the northern and southern continents to the islands in Earth's oceans and seas, a long list of irreplaceable animal species needs the help and protection that only human resources can now provide. This map indicates some of the specific continents, countries, bodies of water, and other world areas referred to in *In Peril: Endangered Animals of the Islands*.

EARTH'S ESSENTIAL WATERS

Our Earth is over 70 percent water. All life on Earth is dependent on the oceans. Without them, the planet would be too hot.

The waters of the world contain hundreds of islands inhabited by a variety of wildlife. Literally thousands of animal **species** inhabit these islands of the world's oceans and seas. But many rare and exotic species are being seriously threatened by **habitat** destruction, pollution, hunting, and fishing. If we don't proceed carefully concerning the animals on oceanic islands and in countries bordering Earth's waters, this precious wildlife will vanish.

The islands of the Atlantic Ocean are home to more than seventy **endangered** species. Most of these rare animals live in the Antilles, the Bahamas, the Cape Verde **archipelago**, and the Canary Islands.

INSECTS

The plight of the rare Haitian swallowtail butterfly, *Papilio aristor,* tells a great deal about the destruction of the **environment** of Haiti, a country located on the western third of the island of Hispaniola. The specimen in the photograph below was found in 1981. The last specimen previously sighted was in 1950. This female is from the gardens of the

▲ The Haitian swallowtail butterfly was last seen on Christmas Eve in 1981.

French Embassy in Port-au-Prince. Since the last century, the habitat of this butterfly has progressively been destroyed by humans, with only a small amount of its forest home left. It is only because the embassy gardens offer an environment much like its natural home that the species may be spared from **extinction**.

AMPHIBIANS AND REPTILES

Costa Rican golden toads, *Bufo periglenes*; green sea turtles, *Chelonia mydas*; Kemp's ridley sea turtles, *Lepidochelys kempii*; olive ridley sea turtles, *Lepidochelys olivacea*; and tortoiseshell hawksbill turtles, *Eretmochelys imbricata*, are endangered. All of these turtles live in

▲ Humans hunt the Cuban crocodile for its skin, which is used to make leather products.

tropical and subtropical seas around the world and are disappearing for various reasons at an alarming rate.

Other endangered reptiles of the Atlantic include the giant anole of Culebra Island, *Anolis roosevelti*; the Anegadan iguana of the Virgin Islands, *Cyclura pinguis*; the St. Croix ground lizard, *Ameiva polops*; the Puerto Rican boa, *Epicrates inornatus*; and the Cuban crocodile, *Crocodylus rhombifer*.

BIRDS

Ivory-billed woodpeckers, *Campephilus principalis*, originally lived in the southeastern U.S. and Cuba. But logging has destroyed their forest habitat. Only a few of these birds remain today in the isolated Cupeyal Cuban forest reserve.

The lark, *Calandrella razae*, is native to Raza Island in the

▲ The lark of Raza Island is already so rare that a drought could push it into extinction.

Cape Verde archipelago off the western coast of Africa. This lark population seems to fluctuate with changing conditions in the climate. The lark inhabits only the volcanic plateau that is situated in the center of Raza Island. The natural vegetation in this area is low and extremely sensitive to drought. At the present time, there are only about fifty lark couples left.

White-tailed laurel pigeons, *Columba junoniae*, are native to the Canary Islands off the

▲ Humans still hunt the white-tailed laurel pigeon although only a few dozen survive today.

northwest coast of Africa. Observations of the laurel pigeon are becoming more and more rare, and the total population is estimated at only about several dozen.

Black-browed woodpeckers of the Bahamas, *Melanerpes superciliaris bahamensis*, may already be extinct. The last recorded sighting of these birds took place more than twenty years ago. The main threat to the black-browed woodpeckers is habitat destruction.

Black oystercatchers, *Haematopus meadewaldoi*, wading birds of the Canary Islands, were last seen in 1968. A small population, however, may still survive.

MAMMALS

Haitian solenodons, *Solenodon paradoxus,* are alarmingly close to extinction. These solenodons are **omnivores**, but they feed mainly on snails and larvae. The shrewlike solenodons have a keen sense of smell that helps them locate their **prey**. Their well-developed claws enable them to dislodge any prey that is buried in tree trunks. The main reasons for the depletion of these animals are **deforestation** and predation by wild cats.

▲ The Haitian solenodon is disappearing along with its forest habitat.

Cuba's most threatened mammal is the solenodon, *Solenodon cubanus*. This solenodon is about the size of a rabbit or a large shrew. It has a long and narrow muzzle, or snout, a practically hairless tail, and stiff fur. The Cuban solenodon is a nocturnal animal that hunts worms and insects on the forest floor. The continual destruction of the solenodon's forest habitat and the steady stream of human settlement are the main reasons for its endangered status.

Hutias are large Cuban land rodents. These animals spend much of their time in nests built in the ground or in tree crevices. The hutia-Conga, or prehensile-tailed hutia, *Capromys pilorides*, is abundant and hunted by humans for food. Other Cuban species, such as the large-eared hutia, *Capromys auritus*; Garrido's hutia,

▲ Cuba's hutia-Conga has been spared overhunting and habitat destruction thus far.

Capromys garridoi; the dwarf hutia, *Capromys nanus*; and the little earth hutia, *Capromys sanfelipensis*, are either endangered or nearly extinct.

10

DARK HORIZON

The islands of the North Pacific include the Galápagos Islands, Japan, Hawaii, and the Mariana Islands.

The British naturalist Charles Darwin made the Galápagos Islands famous. He studied the plants and animals there to develop his theory of **evolution**. This theory states that all living things have evolved from preexisting life-forms. His studies also revealed that similar life-forms change, or adapt, to differences in environment and food supplies. Some of Darwin's most famous studies were done with the finches of the Galápagos Islands.

▲ This Galápagos finch may already be extinct.

▲ Lonesome George of the Galápagos Islands is the last survivor of a species of land tortoise that will become extinct with his passing.

REPTILES

The Galápagos Islands are also home to Lonesome George, a 135-year-old male tortoise. He is the sole survivor of the species *Chelonoidis abingdoni.*

A Galápagos turtle species, *Chelonoidis phantastica*, is also in great danger of disappearing and may even be extinct at this time. The latest clues of its survival appeared in 1966.

Birds

The short-tailed albatross, *Diomedea albatrus,* inhabits the North Pacific. It lives mainly on volcanic islands and builds its nests in cooled volcanic ashes. This bird was almost completely killed off in Japan by feather collectors.

Noguchi's woodpecker, *Sapheopipo noguchii,* on Okinawa Island in Japan, numbers only a few dozen birds. Large forested areas are

▲ The crested drepanis, or honeycreeper, lives on the slopes of the Haleakala Volcano.

necessary for the survival of these birds, but its chances for survival in Japan are low due to deforestation.

The crested drepanis, or honeycreeper, *Palmeria dolei,* disappeared from the Hawaiian island of Molokai in 1907. It exists now only on Maui, on the slopes of the Haleakala Volcano.

▲ The Noguchi's woodpecker is rapidly losing its habitat.

▲ Only one colony of the Japanese crested ibis exists.

Japan's crested ibis, also called the hairy ibis, *Nipponia nippon*, is listed among the rarest species on our planet. It inhabits only the island of Sado in Japan, although it used to inhabit Siberia, Manchuria, part of Tibet, several Japanese islands, and Korea. In 1985, there were fewer than two dozen of these birds, and no young birds could be found. The depletion of the species is due to the massive destruction of the forests where it used to nest. Pollution by mercury and its by-products has also created a threat for the Japanese crested ibis.

The O-o, *Moho braccatus*, of Hawaii is virtually extinct on its native island of Kauai. The main reasons for this situation are loss of habitat, feather hunting by humans, and fierce predation by black rats. The last sighting of this species, a lone male, took place in 1989.

The Ou of Hawaii, *Psittirostra psittacea*, has disappeared from Oahu, Molokai, Lanai, and Maui islands. Its total numbers may still reach several hundreds, but **aviary** diseases and rats pose a permanent threat to the Ou.

Hawaii's Laysan duck, *Anas laysanensis*, had almost disappeared by about 1920

▲ The Ou of Hawaii has already disappeared from many of the islands.

▲ The Hawaiian crow is very sensitive to imported aviary diseases.

Only several dozen Hawaiian crows, *Corvus tropicus*, exist today. They live on the island of Hawaii, and are known to the local people as *alala*. The main reasons for the disappearance of this crow species are destruction of natural habitat and various **imported** aviary diseases.

The puaiohi, *Phaeornis palmeri*, is a native of Kauai Island in Hawaii. It numbers several dozen and inhabits the swampy reserve of Alaka'i. It may soon disappear due to predation by other animals, deforestation, and imported aviary diseases.

due to feather hunters and depletion of food sources by rabbits. The rabbit population was almost eliminated in 1926, and the duck population began to increase again. The Laysan duck is still endangered, however, with fewer than forty animals surviving in 1973.

Mariana Islands ducks, *Anas oustaleti*, have been the victims of habitat destruction and hunting by humans. Although this species once thrived on the islands of Guam, Tinian, Saipan, and Rota, it now probably survives only on Tinian Island.

PARADISE IN DANGER

The lush islands of the South Pacific once provided homes and natural protection for thousands of animal species. But today, due to hunting by both humans and imported animals and the destruction of natural habitat, many native species on island paradises such as the Solomons, Lord Howe Island, Fiji, New Caledonia, Polynesia, the Marquesas, Tahiti, and New Zealand are in grave danger.

BIRDS

The Lord Howe wood rail, *Tricholimnas sylvestris*, was once very abundant on Lord Howe Island of Australia. Although there were about

▲ Habitat destruction is a major problem for the wood rail of Lord Howe Island.

▲ Imported cats pose a major threat to the limicolae.

two hundred couples in 1963, this count has been drastically reduced. The wood rail is endangered mainly because of loss of habitat and hunting by other animals.

The rail, *Rallus poecilopterus*, of Fiji, was considered extinct for most of the twentieth century. It was sighted again in 1973, however. The rail falls victim to mongooses, cats, rats, and the destruction of its forest habitat.

Limicolaes, *Thinornis novaeseelandiae*, live on one of the small islands in the Chatham archipelago off the eastern coast of New Zealand's South Island. Also known as the New Zealand plovers, these birds were once abundant on the North and South islands of New Zealand as well as on most of the Chatham Islands. Only about one hundred limicolaes now exist. The main reason for the decreasing numbers of limicolaes is hunting by cats imported to the island.

The takahe, *Notornis mantelli*, of New Zealand is a large, flightless bird. The total population is about two hundred. In spite of conservation efforts, the takahe remains endangered, probably due to competition for food with imported deer.

▲ The rare takahe eats grass seeds and builds its nest on the ground.

▲ The exotic kagu has a strong bill, pale gray plumage, and a long, loose crest.

The animal symbol of New Caledonia, the kagu, *Rhynochetos jubatus*, is the only representative left of the family Rhynochetidae. The population of this timid and strongly territorial bird is estimated at one thousand, but this number is decreasing rapidly. The main threats to the kagus are loss of habitat and hunting by imported **predators**, such as rats, cats, and dogs.

New Caledonian rails, *Tricholimnas lafresnayanus*, have made very few appearances during the twentieth century. Only one specimen was seen more than seventy years ago. Although hunted by humans and imported predators, a few birds may still survive in the humid island forests.

Black honeyeaters, *Gymnomyza aubryana*, live only on the island of New Caledonia. Just a few hundred of these birds survive today. They are seen in two main regions of the island – Mount Tzumac and the reserve of Blue River.

Imperial pigeons, *Ducula galeata*, of the Marquesas are native to Nukuhiva Island. Despite their protected status as of 1967, humans continue to hunt these birds for food.

▲ Only a few hundred black honeyeaters survive today on New Caledonia.

WILDLIFE IN DISTRESS

The Indian Ocean covers about 20 percent of the world's water surface and includes the islands of Madagascar, the Comoros, the Seychelles, the Maldives, the Mascarenes, and Sri Lanka, among others.

These islands once provided homes to countless species of wildlife, but the once-bountiful landscapes have declined because of drought, erosion, overgrazing by cattle, and forest destruction. As a result, many wildlife species on these islands are now endangered.

▲ The Réunion Island gecko is beautifully colored and endangered.

REPTILES

The angonoka, *Geochelone yniphora*, a Madagascan tortoise, numbers four hundred, at most. This tortoise is currently being bred in captivity.

Rodrigues Island geckos, *Phelsuma edwardnewtonii*, and Réunion Island geckos, *Phelsuma inexpecta*, are near extinction, victims of habitat destruction.

BIRDS

The Mauritius kestrel, *Falco punctatus*, was once one of the rarest birds in the world. There were only six species left in the wild in 1986. The Mauritius kestrel needs a forest environment in which to live. Two hundred years ago, the forest covered almost the entire island. Today, it covers only 1 percent of the island. But because of successful efforts to reproduce the birds in captivity and then

▲ The Mauritius kestrel is a victim of habitat destruction.

▲ Audebert's thick-billed cuckoo has not been observed for the last sixty years.

sechellarum, is only present on Frégate Island, a small islet. The twenty magpies found in 1960 inhabit an area of .77 square miles (2 sq. kilometers). Because the magpie feeds on the ground, it has been the victim of cats.

Madagascan white-eyed ducks, *Aythya innotata*, were

return these birds to the wild, there are now approximately one hundred kestrels in the remaining forest areas of Mauritius.

Audebert's thick-billed cuckoo, *Pachycoccyx audeberti*, of Madagascar was first observed in 1879 and is now endangered.

The singing magpie of the Seychelles, *Copsychus*

▲ The Madagascan white-eyed duck is endangered partly because trout are eating many of the chicks.

abundant in 1930. But today, they may be extinct because of hunting by humans and the introduction of trout into their habitat that eat the chicks.

The red owl, *Tyto soumagnei*, last sighted in 1973, is another Madagascan bird that struggles to survive. Its major threat is deforestation.

▲ The Madagascan red owl may still survive even if sightings have become increasingly rare.

Madagascan serpent eagles, *Eutriorchis astur*, should perhaps already be listed among the species that have disappeared. These birds were described for the first time in 1875. No recent observations reveal they still survive. The **camouflage** colors of their **plumage**, however, make these birds difficult to spot in the forest.

MAMMALS

A Madagascan primate called the aye-aye, *Daubentonia madagascariensis*, is about the size of a cat. The aye-aye has a slender third toe equipped with a special claw. This claw enables it to dig for the fruit pulp and insect larvae that make up its diet. The greatest dangers to the aye-ayes are hunting by

▲ There are only a few aye-ayes left on Madagascar.

humans, imported predators, and deforestation. In 1965, there were about fifty aye-ayes on Madagascar. The greatest chance for survival of the species is the reserve of Nossi-Mangabé. Miraculously, some of the forest cover on this small island has not been disturbed.

The indri, *Indri indri*, of Madagascar is a peaceful primate threatened with extinction. This large gray-and-black lemur leaps and clings to lush foliage and trees as it moves through the tropical rain forests of the island. The main threat to the indri is large-scale habitat destruction.

Sifakas, *Propithecus verreauxi*, of Madagascar are also near extinction due to hunting. The most threatened subspecies, *Propithecus verreauxi coronatus*, has only a few hundred specimens.

▲ The endangered indri of Madagascar.

The list of animals in danger on the oceanic islands is growing at an alarming rate. The species mentioned in this book are but a few of those approaching extinction.

It is very important that we act today to protect these animals and their endangered habitats. Every effort to save animal and plant species and their habitat is valuable because no living thing exists on its own. We are all part of the balance of nature.

▲ The sifaka is an endangered herbivore that eats leaves, flowers, fruits, and tree bark.

SCIENTIFIC NAMES OF ANIMALS IN THIS BOOK

Animals have different names in every language. To simplify matters, researchers the world over have agreed to use the same scientific names, usually from ancient Greek or Latin, to identify animals. With this in mind, most animals are classified by two names. One is the genus name; the other is the name of the species to which they belong. Additional names indicate further subgroupings. The scientific names for the animals included in *In Peril: Endangered Animals of the Islands* are:

Anegadan iguana . . . . *Cyclura pinguis*
Angonoka . . . . *Geochelone yniphora*
Audebert's thick billed cuckoo
. . . . *Pachycoccyx audeberti*
Aye-aye . . . . *Daubentonia madagascariensis*
Black honeyeater . . . . *Gymnomyza aubryana*
Black oystercatcher . . . *Haematopus meadewaldoi*
Black-browed woodpecker
. . . . *Melanerpes superciliaris bahamensis*
Costa Rican golden toad . . . . *Bufo periglenes*
Crested drepanis . . . . *Palmeria dolei*
Cuban crocodile . . . . *Crocodylus rhombifer*
Cuban solenodon . . . . *Solenodon cubanus*
Dwarf hutia . . . .*Capromys nanus*
Earth hutia . . . . *Capromys sanfelipensis*
Fiji rail . . . . *Rallus poecilopterus*
Galápagos finch
. . . . *Geospiza magnirostris magnirostris*
Galápagos tortoise . . . . . . *Chelonoidis abingdoni*
Galápagos turtle. . . . . . . *Chelonoidis phantastica*
Garrido's hutia . . . . *Capromys garridoi*
Giant anole . . . . *Anolis roosevelti*
Green sea turtle . . . . *Chelonia mydas*
Haitian solenodon . . . . . . *Solenodon paradoxus*
Haitian swallowtail butterfly . . . . . *Papilio aristor*
Hawaiian crow . . . . *Corvus tropicus*
Hutia-Conga . . . . *Capromys pilorides*
Imperial pigeon . . . .*Ducula galeata*
Indri . . . . *Indri indri*
Ivory-billed woodpecker . *Campephilus principalis*

Japanese crested ibis . . . . *Nipponia nippon*
Kagu . . . . *Rhynochetos jubatus*
Kemp's ridley sea turtle . . . . . *Lepidochelys kempii*
Large-eared hutia . . . . *Capromys auritus*
Laysan duck . . . . *Anas laysanensis*
Limicolae . . . . *Thinornis novaeseelandiae*
Lord Howe wood rail . . . . *Tricholimnas sylvestris*
Madagascan white-eyed duck . . . *Aythya innotata*
Mariana Islands duck . . . . *Anas oustaleti*
Mauritius kestrel . . . . *Falco punctatus*
New Caledonian rail . *Tricholimnas lafresnayanus*
Noguchi's woodpecker . . . . *Sapheopipo noguchii*
Olive ridley sea turtle . . . . . *Lepidochelys olivacea*
O-o . . . . *Moho braccatus*
Ou . . . . *Psittirostra psittacea*
Puaiohi . . . . *Phaeornis palmeri*
Puerto Rican boa . . . . *Epicrates inornatus*
Raza Island lark . . . . *Calandrella razae*
Red owl . . . . *Tyto soumagnei*
Réunion Island gecko . . . . . *Phelsuma inexpecta*
Rodrigues Island gecko *Phelsuma edwardnewtonii*
Serpent eagle . . . .*Eutriorchis astur*
Short-tailed albatross . . . . *Diomedea albatrus*
Sifaka . . . . *Propithecus verreauxi coronatus*
Singing magpie . . . . *Copsychus sechellarum*
St. Croix ground lizard . . . . *Ameiva polops*
Takahe . . . . *Notornis mantelli*
Tortoiseshell hawksbill turtle . . . .
. . . .*Eretmochelys imbricata*
White-tailed laurel pigeon . . . . *Columba junoniae*

GLOSSARY

archipelago — a large group of islands.

aviary — a place where birds are confined.

camouflage — to hide, conceal, or disguise. The color and markings of certain animals hide, or camouflage, them from enemies by helping them blend into their surroundings.

deforestation — to cut down or clear out the trees in a forest.

endangered — in peril or danger of dying out, or becoming extinct.

environment — the surroundings in which animals and plants live.

evolution — a gradual change or development over a long period of time.

extinction — the dying out of all members of a plant or animal species.

habitat — an environment where plants and animals live and grow.

imported — brought in from a foreign place or an outside source.

omnivores — animals that eat both plants and other animals.

plumage — the entire covering of feathers of a bird.

predators — animals that kill other animals for food.

prey — an animal that is eaten by another animal for food.

species — a grouping of animals with the same physical attributes.

MORE BOOKS TO READ

A Kid's Guide to How to Save the Planet. Billy Goodman (Avon)

Conservation Directory. (National Wildlife Federation)

Lost Wild Worlds. Robert M. McClung (William Morrow)

Meant to Be Wild. Jan DeBlieu (Fulcrum)

Save the Earth. Betty Miles (Knopf)

Saving Animals: The World Wildlife Book of Conservation. Bernard Stonehouse (Macmillan)

Why Are Whales Vanishing? Isaac Asimov (Gareth Stevens)

VIDEOTAPES

Call or visit your local library or video rental store to see if these videotapes are available for your viewing.

The Dragons of Galápagos. (The Undersea World of Jacques Cousteau)

The Forgotten Mermaids. (The Undersea World of Jacques Cousteau)

The Great Whales. (National Geographic)

The Humpbacks of Maui. (Pacific Whale Foundation)

PLACES TO WRITE

The following organizations work to educate people about animals, promote the protection of animals, and encourage the conservation of their environments. If you write for more information, be sure to state clearly what you want to know.

Division of Endangered
   Species
U.S. Fish and Wildlife
   Service
452 Arlington Square
Washington, D.C. 20240

Sea Shepherd Conservation
   Society (Canada)
P.O. Box 48446
Vancouver,
British Columbia V7X 1A2

International Wildlife
   Coalition
P.O. Box 461
Port Credit Postal Station
Mississauga, Ontario
L5G 4M1

New South Wales National
   Parks and Wildlife
   Service Information
   Centre
43 Bridge Street
(P.O. Box 1967)
Hurstville NSW 2220
Australia

Conservation Commission
   of the Northern
   Territory
P.O. Box 496
Palmerston
NT 0831
Australia

Wildlife Conservation
   International
185th Street and Southern
   Boulevard
Bronx, New York 10460

ACTIVITIES TO HELP SAVE ENDANGERED SPECIES

1. Write the United States Department of the Interior, Publications Unit, Fish and Wildlife Service, Washington, D.C., 20240, for a list of endangered wildlife. Then write to government officials and express your support for the protection of these animals and their habitat. Also, write to government officials to express your support for strengthening the Endangered Species Act.

2. Contact a nature organization in your area. Ask how you can become involved in helping save wildlife.

3. Do not buy wild or exotic animals as pets. Also, do not buy fur, bearskin rugs, ivory, or any other products that endanger animals.

4. Contact a wildlife rehabilitation center in your area and find out what educational programs or activities it offers to the public.

5. Educate your friends about respecting wildlife. Ask them not to participate in acts of carelessness or cruelty that could injure an animal.

INDEX